For information about this title or to order other books
and/or electronic media, contact the publisher:
Joqlie Publishing, LLC
www.joqliepublishing.com

ISBN: 978-1-957875-57-6

Printed in the United States of America

Cover and Interior Design: Joqlie Publishing, LLC

The One Action System – Empowering ADHD Kids to Thrive One Task at a Time

By Dawn Callahan

For those who have ADHD and the people who love them

Book Contents

Introduction

As a parent of a child with ADHD, I know how challenging it can be to get them to complete even the simplest of tasks. The constant distractions, the restlessness, the struggle to focus—it can all feel overwhelming. But I discovered a One Action System that has been a game-changer for us.

The key is to make the task so simple and straightforward that it requires minimal effort and attention. For example, instead of asking my son to clean his room, I'll say, "Go put your dirty clothes in the hamper." That's it—just one small, specific action. Framing the task in this direct, one action way removes the overwhelming feeling of a bigger project and makes it easier for the child to focus and follow through.

The beauty of this approach is that it plays to the strengths of ADHD kids. They excel at focusing on simple, immediate tasks. By removing the overwhelming nature of bigger projects, you harness their ability to stay engaged for short bursts. Plus, the sense of accomplishment from checking off each mini-task provides positive reinforcement to keep going.

I know it can be tempting to give up and do everything yourself, but resist that urge. With patience and this One Action System, you can empower your ADHD child to develop essential life skills and independence. It may take longer, but you'll be amazed at what they can achieve.

Dawn

Chapter 1
ADHD and the Challenges of Multi-Step Tasks

Here is a scenario of how multi-step tasks can be challenging from the perspective of a child with ADHD:

"It was time to get ready for school, but I just couldn't seem to focus. My mom kept telling me the steps - get dressed, brush your teeth, and pack your backpack. But as soon as she'd finished listing them, I'd forget half of what she said.

I'd start getting dressed, then suddenly remember I needed to brush my teeth. So I'd run to the bathroom, only to realize I forgot to put on my socks. Back and forth I went, jumping from one task to the next without completing any of them.

My mom would gently remind me of the steps, but by that point, I was already flustered and overwhelmed. The more she tried to help, the more frustrated I got. Why couldn't I just do these simple things in the right order?

When it was time to pack my backpack, I'd grab my books and folders, then get distracted by a toy on my shelf. Before I knew it, I'd be playing instead of packing. My mom would have to come in and walk me through it step-by-step.

I felt so stupid and incapable, watching my friends breeze through their morning routines. Why did these multi-step tasks have to be so hard for me? I just wanted to be able to do them on my own without constantly forgetting.

As we rushed out the door, already running late, my mom gave me an encouraging smile. "It's okay, buddy. We'll work on it together. One action at a time." Her patience helped me feel a little better, but I couldn't help wishing my brain worked the way everyone else's did."

When children with ADHD consistently fail to follow through, it can lead to a sense of frustration, low self-esteem, and falling behind academically and socially.

The cognitive and behavioral symptoms of ADHD can make it extremely difficult for these children to complete tasks that involve multiple steps. Completing tasks, whether getting ready in the morning, finishing homework, or doing chores, is a life skill necessary through adulthood.

Chapter 2
What is the One Action System?

As I mentioned, the One Action System is a structured approach that breaks down multi-step tasks into single, manageable actions. By focusing on completing one action at a time, children with ADHD can build the skills and confidence needed to tackle more complex tasks.

But the One Action System is more than just task breakdown - it also incorporates visual cues and routine-building. Using the One Action System, I created a series of illustrated checklists to guide my son through his daily routines, from getting ready in the morning to completing homework in the evening. These checklists serve as a constant, reassuring reference point, reducing the mental effort required to remember what needs to be done.

Consistency is key, so we've established a predictable schedule and environment for these routines. My son knows exactly when and where certain tasks will happen, allowing him to focus on the action at hand without feeling overwhelmed by the bigger picture.

Implementing this system has resulted in my son having a newfound sense of control and pride in his abilities. Homework is completed on time, chores are done without constant reminders, and morning and bedtime routines run smoothly.

Chapter 3
Implementing the One Action System

There are 4 steps to implementing the One Action System. Let's review each step in more detail.

Step 1: Identify Target Tasks

Begin by selecting appropriate tasks to target, taking into account your child's age, developmental level, and specific ADHD-related challenges.

Look for tasks that meet the following criteria:

- Discrete and Measurable: The task should have a clear beginning and end, with easily identifiable actions. This makes it easier for your child to understand what's expected and track their progress.

- Appropriate Difficulty Level: The task should be challenging enough to be meaningful, but not so difficult that it becomes overwhelming. Start with tasks that are within your child's current capabilities, and gradually increase the complexity as they gain confidence and skills.

- Relevant to Daily Life: Choose tasks that are directly relevant to your child's daily routines and responsibilities, such as getting ready in the morning, completing homework, or helping with chores. This will help them see the immediate value and importance of mastering these skills.

- Engaging and Motivating: Select tasks that align with your child's interests and strengths, or that offer a sense of accomplishment and pride upon completion. This will help maintain their motivation and engagement throughout the process.

*Remember, the One Action System is all about setting your child up for success!

Step 2: Break Down the Task

Carefully analyze the target task and break it down into its most basic, single-action components. This may involve creating visual checklists, using physical cues, or finding other ways to make each action clear and concrete.

Let's say the task is cleaning their bedroom. That may seem straightforward to us, but for a child with ADHD, it can quickly become overwhelming.

First, I would sit down by myself and carefully analyze the task. I'll think about all the actions involved - from clearing the surfaces to making the bed and putting away toys and clothes and write them down. I'll make a visual checklist from this list, using simple icons or words to represent each action.

The key is to break it down to the most basic, single-action components. Instead of saying "Clean your room," I'll say "Let's put your books away." Once that's done, we'll move on to the next action, celebrating the small victories along the way.

Step 3: Teach the One Action System

Begin by explaining the rationale behind the One Action System to your child. You can say, "You know how sometimes it can feel overwhelming to look at a big project or chore and not know where to start? The One Action System will help make those tasks feel more manageable."

Emphasize that the key is to focus on the next action, rather than trying to plan the entire task from start to finish. This helps prevent your child from feeling paralyzed by the bigger picture.

Next, introduce physical cues to make each action even clearer. For example, you might place a laundry basket in the middle of the room to indicate where all the dirty clothes should go. Or set out cleaning supplies in a designated spot to show where they need to start

Next, model how to use the One Action System for your child. Walk them through the below:

1. Identify the task that needs to be done. For example, "Cleaning your room."

2. Ask yourself, "What is the very next physical action I need to take?" In this case, it might be "Pick up the dirty clothes on the floor."

3. Do that one action and only that action. Don't worry about the rest of the task yet.

4. Once that first action is complete, ask yourself again: "What is the next physical action?"

Provide plenty of encouragement as your child practices this new approach. Remember to celebrate each small victory, reminding them that completing one action at a time is the key to tackling bigger tasks.

Step 4: Implement and Reinforce

After establishing the One Action System with your child, the key is to consistently implement and reinforce the process. This will help them internalize the actions and make it a natural part of their task management routine.

Begin by setting up visual prompts and reminders around the home. Post checklists on the fridge put sticky notes on their desk or create a digital calendar with alerts. These cues will continuously guide your child through the One Action System.

Provide plenty of encouragement and praise when you observe them using the system correctly. Celebrate small victories, like remembering to check the checklist or breaking a big task into smaller actions. This positive reinforcement will motivate them to keep up with the new habit.

You may also want to incorporate rewards, such as stickers, small treats, or privileges when they demonstrate consistent use of the One Action System. This extrinsic motivation can go a long way, especially in the beginning stages.

Throughout this implementation phase, monitor your child's progress closely. Are they remembering to refer to the checklists? Are they breaking down tasks effectively? Identify any areas that need more support or tweaking of the system.

Don't be afraid to make adjustments as needed. The One Action System should evolve to best suit your child's individual needs and learning style.

Chapter 4
Customizing the One Action System

Adapting for Different Ages and Developmental Levels
What is great about the One Action System is its flexibility to be tailored for children at any age or developmental stage. Whether working with a young elementary student or a high school teen, the core principles remain the same - providing a simple, structured approach to task management. However, the specific implementation will need to be adjusted based on the child's cognitive abilities, attention span, and level of independence.

- Elementary School (Grades K-5)

  For younger children, the One Action System should be kept as visual and hands-on as possible. Use large, colorful checklists with simple icons or pictures to represent each task. Break down multi-step assignments into single, concrete actions that can be checked off. Provide frequent adult guidance and supervision to ensure tasks are being completed. Celebrate small victories and use positive reinforcement liberally.

- Middle School (Grades 6-8)

  As children reach the middle school years, they can begin taking on more responsibility for their task management. Introduce written checklists and schedules, but still keep them uncluttered and easy to reference. Allow for more independence, but maintain regular check-ins to provide support and troubleshoot any issues. Teach organizational and time management skills to build their executive functioning abilities.

- High School (Grades 9-12)

   High school students are ready for a more sophisticated One Action System. Encourage them to take the lead in designing their customized tools, whether digital or analog. Focus on fostering self-awareness, metacognition (i.e. being aware and understanding of your thought process), and the ability to self-monitor and self-correct. Gradually release responsibility but remain available as a coach and mentor to help them navigate the increasing academic and extracurricular demands.

*The key with all ages is to meet the child where they are and make incremental progress.

Addressing Specific ADHD Symptoms
By understanding your child's specific ADHD symptoms, you can modify the system to provide the support they need. Below are some tips to help with specific symptoms associated with ADHD.

- Impulsivity:

   Children with ADHD often struggle with impulsivity, making it difficult for them to pause and think before acting. To address this, incorporate visual cues into the One Action System. For example, use a stop sign or a red light to signal your child to stop and think before moving to the next action. Encourage them to take a deep breath and consider their options before proceeding.

- Difficulty with Transitions:

Transitions can be particularly challenging for children with ADHD, as they may have trouble shifting their focus and attention. To ease these transitions, provide clear, instructions for moving from one task to the next. Offer reminders and praise when they successfully complete the transition.

- Struggles with Working Memory:

  ADHD can also impact a child's working memory, making it difficult for them to remember and follow multi-action instructions. Encourage them to repeat the actions back to you to reinforce the information.

Chapter 5
Expanding the One Action System

Generalizing to Other Tasks
As your child becomes more comfortable and proficient with the One Action System for certain tasks, it's time to start applying the same principles to a wider range of activities. This gradual expansion will help your child build confidence and competence in managing their responsibilities.

The key is to start simple and slowly increase the complexity as your child demonstrates mastery. Begin by identifying other daily or weekly tasks that could benefit from the one action system, such as:

- Packing a school bag

- Cleaning an area of the house

- Completing homework assignments

- Preparing a simple meal

- Doing laundry

- Yard work or gardening

For each new task, break it down into a single, clear action that your child can focus on. Provide visual aids, checklists, or reminders as needed to support their understanding and execution.

As your child completes these one action tasks, you can then introduce additional actions or layers of complexity. For example, with packing a school bag, you might start with "Put your homework in your bag" and then expand to "Put your homework in your bag, then zip it closed."

The goal is to empower your child to generalize the one action system to a variety of situations.

Fostering Independence
As your child becomes more comfortable with the One Action System, you should help them internalize the approach and apply it independently to new situations. This transition towards self-regulation and independent task completion is crucial for long-term success.

One key strategy is to gradually reduce your direct involvement and guidance. Start by having your child walk through the One Action System aloud, verbalizing each stage. This reinforces the mental framework and helps cement the actions. Gradually fade your prompts, allowing them to go through it silently on their own.

Next, encourage your child to initiate the One Action System unprompted when faced with a new task or challenge. Praise and reward this self-starting behavior, as it demonstrates growing independence. You can also have them teach the system to a sibling or friend, which solidifies their understanding.

As your child becomes more adept, start introducing more complex, multi-action tasks. Guide them through breaking it down into discrete actions. Over time, step back and let them tackle the decomposition on their own, only intervening if they get stuck.

Fostering a growth mindset is also important. Emphasize that the One Action System is a tool they can adapt and apply flexibly. Celebrate their creativity in finding new ways to use it. Encourage them to experiment and problem-solve when facing novel challenges.

Chapter 6
Addressing Challenges, Setbacks, and Maintaining Progress

Addressing Challenges and Setbacks

Even with the One Action System in place, your child may still encounter obstacles along the way. It's important to be prepared to identify and overcome common challenges to ensure continued progress.

- Resistance

    One of the most common challenges is resistance from your child. They may be reluctant to engage with the One Action System, either due to a lack of understanding or a preference for old habits. To address this, take time to clearly explain the benefits of the new approach and involve your child in the process. Encourage them to provide feedback and make adjustments as needed to ensure the system works for them.

- Frustration

    As your child works to build new habits, they may experience frustration when progress seems slow or they encounter setbacks. Validate their feelings and remind them that change takes time. Encourage them to persist through difficult moments. Provide additional support to help maintain motivation.

- Difficulty Maintaining Motivation

  Sustaining motivation can be a challenge, especially when the novelty of the One Action System wears off. Regularly review your child's goals and progress, and adjust the system as needed to keep them engaged. Incorporate their interests and preferences to make the process more enjoyable. Encourage them to track their own progress and celebrate milestones, which can help maintain a sense of accomplishment.

- Overcoming Obstacles

  When faced with challenges, it's important to approach them with patience and flexibility. Collaborate with your child to identify the root cause of the problem and develop a plan to address it. This may involve modifying the One Action System, providing additional support, or addressing underlying issues such as stress or anxiety.

*Remember, setbacks are a natural part of the change process. The key is to view them as opportunities for growth and learning, rather than failures. Encourage your child to reflect on what they've learned and how they can apply that knowledge to overcome future obstacles.

Sustaining Long-Term Success

Maintaining progress with the One Action System requires ongoing support and reinforcement. Let's review practical strategies to weave the approach into your child's daily routine, and collaborate effectively with teachers and other caregivers.

- Weaving the One Action System into Daily Life

  Consistency is key when implementing the One Action System. Work to integrate the system seamlessly into your child's daily activities at home, school, and beyond by:

  - Posting visual cues and reminders in key locations to prompt the One Action System.

  - Role-play common scenarios and practice the One Action System together.

  - Narrate your own use of the One Action System as you model it for your child.

  - Incorporate the language and structure into everyday conversations and tasks.

- Collaborating with Teachers and Caregivers

  Aligning your child's support system is crucial. Regularly communicate with teachers, therapists, and other adults in your child's life to ensure everyone is on the same page.

  - Schedule meetings to explain the One Action System and get buy-in.

  - Provide clear instructions and visual aids for implementing the system.

  - Coordinate consistent language, cues, and reinforcement across all environments.

- Check in frequently to troubleshoot challenges and celebrate progress.

- Celebrating Successes

  Regularly acknowledge and reward your child's efforts, no matter how small. This positive reinforcement will help solidify the new habits.

  - Create a visual progress tracker to mark milestones.

  - Plan special outings or activities as rewards for achieving goals.

  - Share success stories with family, teachers, and support networks.

  - Express genuine pride in your child's hard work and growth.

Finally, be patient and trust the process! Developing this new skill will take practice. However, with repetition, the One Action System will become a natural habit. Your child will start to see that breaking things down into manageable pieces makes previously daunting tasks feel much more doable.

Closing Thoughts

I hope this book was helpful for you and offered additional tools to help you and your child with ADHD. Since implementing the One Action System across all areas of my son's life—homework, chores, even playtime—I've watched him tackle increasingly complex challenges with focus and determination. Of course, there are still challenges, but I learned to be patient, to adjust the actions as needed, and to listen to my son.

If you're a parent struggling to help your child with ADHD, know that you are not alone. I understand and support you and am cheering on you and your wonderful child with your journey.

About

Dawn, an avid reader and outdoor enthusiast, is a passionate advocate for ADHD awareness. From her home in the sunbelt, she works to bring greater understanding and support to those living with ADHD.

Connect with Dawn

Email: customersupport@joqliepublishing.com

Facebook: @joqliepublishing

Instagram: @joqliepublishing